A Day with Police Officers

By Jan Kottke

Welcome Books

SCHOLASTIC INC.

New York Toronto London Auckland Sydney
Mexico City New Delhi Hong Kong Buenos Aires

Photo Credits: Cover, p. 5, 7, 9, 13, 17, 21 by Thaddeus Harden;
p. 11 © FPG; p. 15, 19 © Corbis
Contributing Editor: Jennifer Ceaser
Book Design: Michael DeLisio

ISBN 0-516-24523-6

23 22 21   17 18 19/0

Printed in China.   62

First Scholastic printing, September 2002

Scholastic Inc., 557 Broadway, New York, NY 10012.

Contents

We are **police officers**.

We help people.

We keep people safe.

4

5

We start our day at the **police station**.

We find out where we will **patrol** that day.

I patrol the roads.

I make sure people don't break the **law**.

I have to write a **ticket** if a person drives too fast.

9

We patrol on horses.

There's a big **parade** today.

We make sure that people march safely.

I patrol on a boat.

I make sure that everyone is being safe in the water.

I patrol on a bike.

I ride my bike through the park.

I make sure everyone in the park is safe.

15

I work in the street.

I use my hands to tell cars when to stop and go.

I make sure people cross the street safely.

I patrol with Buster.

Buster is a police dog.

Buster helps me look for **clues**.

19

Sometimes I stop and talk to people.

They thank me for keeping them safe.

I'm happy to help them.

21

New Words

clues (klooz) things that help police figure out when someone has done something wrong

law (law) a rule that people must follow

parade (puh-**rayd**) a group of people that march together down a street

patrol (puh-**trol**) to keep a place safe

police officers (puh-**leese aw**-fih-sirz) people who make sure others are safe and follow laws

police station (puh-**leese stay**-shen) a place where police officers work

ticket (**tik**-it) something given to a driver who breaks the law

To Find Out More

Books
Officer Brown Keeps Neighborhoods Safe
by Alice K. Flanagan
Children's Press

Web Site
Super Trooper
http://www.users.fast.net/~louis2/index.html
This site has information about police officers and the equipment they use.
It also includes important safety tips.

Index

About the Author

Jan Kottke is the owner/director of several preschools in the Tidewater area of Virginia. A lifelong early education professional, she is completing a phonics reading series for preschoolers.

Reading Consultants

Kris Flynn, Coordinator, Small School District Literacy, The San Diego County Office of Education

Shelly Forys, Certified Reading Recovery Specialist, W.J. Zahnow Elementary School, Waterloo, IL

Peggy McNamara, Professor, Bank Street College of Education, Reading and Literacy Program